CRA

CRANBERRIES

By
Sherri Eldridge

Illustrations by
Rob Groves

Published by:
Harvest Hill Press
P.O. Box 55
Salisbury Cove, Maine 04672
207-288-8900

ISBN: 1-886862-15-X

First printing: June 1997
Second printing: August 1998
Third printing: August 2001
Fourth printing: April 2002

PRINTED IN CANADA
ON ACID-FREE PAPER

The recipes in this book were created with the goal of reducing fat, calories, cholesterol and sodium. They also present a variety of fresh healthy foods, to be prepared with love and eaten with pleasure.

CREDITS:

Cover: Cotton print border gratefully used as a courtesy of:
Judie Rothermel

Cover Design, Layout and Typesetting: Sherri Eldridge

Front Cover Watercolor and Text Line Art: Robert Groves

Text Typesetting and Proofreading: Bill Eldridge

PREFACE

Cranberries grow in both North America and Europe. The North American cranberry is larger than its cousins, the English fenberry and the Scandinavian lingonberry. Native Americans called the cranberry ibimi, meaning "bitter berry."

True cranberries grow in peat and sand bogs, although there are highbush hybrids that can be grown on less soggy land. By mid-October the cranberry bogs are a vibrant red and are ready to be harvested. The sight of fresh cranberries in the market is a harbinger of the holiday season.

Besides the traditional cranberry relish, cranberries are excellent in baked goods such as muffins, pancakes, breads and even as an accent in fruit pies. A refreshing glass of cranberry juice can even help cure or prevent certain illnesses.

The beautiful bags of bright cranberries invite you to explore the varied uses of cranberries in this book. And while the beautiful red berries are fresh and plentiful, put a few bags in the freezer to enjoy all year round!

CONTENTS

Cranberry Buttermilk Pancakes

SERVES 6

1 cup cranberries, washed
and chopped
½ cup sugar
2 cups flour
2 teaspoons baking powder
1 egg
1 egg white
2 cups lowfat buttermilk
3 tablespoons honey
3 tablespoons canola oil

Serving: 3 Pancakes	Calories: 354
Protein: 8 gm	Fat: 8.5 gm
Carbs: 61 gm	Cholesterol: 38 mg
Sodium: 240 mg	Calcium: 161 mg

Mash chopped cranberries with sugar and set aside.

In a large bowl, sift together dry ingredients. In a separate bowl, beat egg until fluffy, then add buttermilk, honey and oil. Make a well in dry ingredients and slowly pour in buttermilk mixture. Stir just enough to combine.

Spray preheated griddle with nonstick oil. Ladle batter onto griddle. Sprinkle with cranberries. Turn pancakes when half the bubbles burst, and briefly cook on the other side until golden.

Cranberry Waffles

1 cup fresh cranberries
½ cup sugar
1½ cups nonfat yogurt
1½ cups nonfat cottage
    cheese
1½ cups lowfat buttermilk
1 teaspoon vanilla
2 cups all-purpose flour
1 tablespoon baking powder
3 egg whites

SERVES 6

Finely chop cranberries, then mix with sugar. Purée yogurt and cottage cheese in blender for 4 minutes. Transfer to bowl, stir in buttermilk and vanilla. Sift together flour and baking powder. Whip into buttermilk mixture. Stir in sugared cranberries.

Beat egg whites to soft peaks and fold into batter. Cook in preheated waffle iron sprayed with nonstick oil.

Serving: 1 Waffle
Protein: 11 gm
Carbs: 58 gm
Sodium: 289 mg

Calories: 282
Fat: 0.5 gm
Cholesterol: 1 mg
Calcium: 184 mg

Cranberry Syrup

1 cup cranberries
2 cups water
2 cups maple syrup
1 cinnamon stick

Serving: 2 Tablespoons
Protein: 0 gm
Carbs: 21 gm
Sodium: 4 mg

Calories: 80
Fat: 0 gm
Cholesterol: 0 mg
Calcium: 33 mg

MAKES 2½ CUPS

Boil cranberries in water until soft. Drain in fine sieve, then mash cranberry pulp through sieve and return to cooking pot. Add maple syrup and cinnamon stick to cranberry pulp. Warm over medium-low heat for 10 minutes. Serve hot over waffles or pancakes.

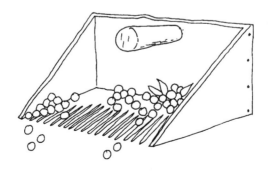

Cranberry Square Crisp

SERVES 9

2 cups chopped fresh or
dried cranberries
¼ cup chopped walnuts
1½ cups sugar
1 egg white
⅓ cup skim milk
3 tablespoons melted butter
1 cup flour
pinch of salt
1 teaspoon vanilla or
almond extract

Preheat oven to 350°. Spray 9-inch square baking pan with nonstick oil.

Mix cranberries, walnuts and ½ cup of the sugar. Spread in baking pan.

Mix together remaining cup of sugar and all other ingredients. Stir until smooth. Pour over cranberries. Bake 40 minutes or until top crust becomes light golden brown. Cool 30 minutes. Cut into 3-inch squares.

Serving: 1 Square
Protein: 2 gm
Carbs: 36 gm
Sodium: 49 mg

Calories: 191
Fat: 4.5 gm
Cholesterol: 8 mg
Calcium: 14 mg

Warm Cranberry Pudding

SERVES 8

1 cup wheat berries
2 cups chopped cranberries
1 cup sugar
1 cup honey
4 cups skim milk
2 teaspoons cinnamon
1 cup chopped dried apples
2 teaspoons finely grated
    lemon rind
pinch of salt
1 egg
2 egg whites
1 teaspoon vanilla

Serving: 1/8 Recipe
Protein: 7 gm
Carbs: 83 gm
Sodium: 112 mg

Calories: 351
Fat: 1 gm
Cholesterol: 29 mg
Calcium: 171 mg

Soak wheat berries in water. In a separate bowl, mix cranberries with sugar and honey. Let both bowls sit overnight.

Drain wheat berries, then boil with 4 cups water for 30 minutes, drain. Add milk and cinnamon. Simmer 35 minutes. Stir in cranberries, apples, grated lemon rind and salt.

Preheat oven to 325°. Spray and 8"x8" casserole with nonstick oil.

Whisk together egg, egg whites and vanilla. Stir in small amount of wheat berry mixture. Beat egg mixture into remaining wheat berries. Pour into casserole, and bake 35 minutes.

Cranberries in the Garden

True cranberries prefer to grow in bogs, and can be difficult to cultivate in a garden. However, there is a substitute cranberry which comes from the viburnum family. These viburnums are called the highbush cranberry.

The highbush cranberry is a lovely ornamental shrub that can grow to twelve feet tall. With showy white flowers, its blooms are as large as four inches wide. The highbush cranberry is winter hardy, prefers moist loamy soils, and is easy to grow. Its berries do not have as full a flavor as a real cranberry, but they can still be used in relishes, baked goods and preserves.

Some varieties of true cranberries can be grown without a bog. The southern cranberry and lingonberry are both happy in moist loamy soils. These both produce a smaller crop than the larger American cranberry, but still have a full cranberry flavor.

For the determined gardener and cranberry lover, a low-lying area can be prepared with layers of peat and sand to create the acidic soil of a bog. Plantings can be taken from cuttings, which will sprout from either end of the vine. Given a cool growing season and ample water, you too can harvest your own!

Cinnamon-Orange
Cranberry Sauce

1 lb. fresh cranberries

1 cup orange juice

1 ½ cups packed brown sugar

1 teaspoon cinnamon

1 teaspoon finely grated
   orange rind

Wash cranberries. Cook in orange juice until the skins burst, and continue to cook 5 minutes more. Stir in sugar, cinnamon and orange rind. Serve warm or chill to firm for a traditional cranberry sauce.

Serving: 1/4 Cup
Protein: 0 gm
Carbs: 45 gm
Sodium: 17 mg

Calories: 177
Fat: 0 gm
Cholesterol: 0 mg
Calcium: 43 mg

Cranberry-Nut Muffins

MAKES 12 MUFFINS

1 cup chopped fresh or
    dried cranberries
¾ cup sugar
3 tablespoons chopped
    walnuts
1¾ cups all-purpose flour
1 tablespoon baking powder
½ teaspoon baking soda
1 teaspoon cinnamon
1 teaspoon ground ginger
1 egg
1½ tablespoons canola oil
1 cup lowfat buttermilk
1 teaspoon almond extract

Preheat oven to 400°. Lightly spray muffin tins with nonstick oil.

Mix cranberries with sugar and nuts, set aside. Sift together flour, baking powder, baking soda and spices. In a separate bowl, beat together remaining ingredients. With a few swift strokes, combine the three mixtures (some lumps will remain).

Fill cups of muffin tins ¾ full. Bake 20 minutes or until a toothpick inserted in the center of muffins comes out clean.

Serve muffins while still warm.

Serving: 1 Muffin
Protein: 3 gm
Carbs: 29 gm
Sodium: 163 mg

Calories: 160
Fat: 3.5 gm
Cholesterol: 18 mg
Calcium: 56 mg

Cranberry Orange Muffins

1 orange
2 tablespoons canola oil
¾ cup packed brown sugar
1 egg
1 egg white
1 cup skim milk
2 cups all-purpose flour
2 tablespoons baking powder
1 cup chopped fresh or
    dried cranberries
3 tablespoons chopped
    pecans

Serving: 1 Muffin
Protein: 4 gm
Carbs: 33 gm
Sodium: 226 mg

Calories: 182
Fat: 4 gm
Cholesterol: 18 mg
Calcium: 128 mg

MAKES 12 MUFFINS

Preheat oven to 400°. Lightly spray muffin tins with nonstick oil.

Grate orange rind, peel orange to pulp and scoop out pulp. Reserve any juice.

Cream oil and sugar. Beat in eggs, milk and any orange juice. In a separate bowl, stir flour and baking powder together. With a few quick strokes, stir flour, orange rind, orange pulp, cranberries and pecans into liquid mixture. Spoon into muffin tins and bake for 25 minutes or until a toothpick inserted in the center of muffins comes out clean. Serve warm.

Quick
Cranberry-Carrot Bread

1½ cups grated carrots
1 cup chopped fresh or
   dried cranberries
1 cup packed brown sugar
3 tablespoons honey
1 teaspoon lemon juice
1 teaspoon baking soda
3 tablespoons safflower oil
3 tablespoons poppy seeds
1 cup boiling water
2 cups all-purpose flour
2 teaspoons baking powder
1 teaspoon cinnamon

Serving: 1 Slice
Protein: 3 gm
Carbs: 41 gm
Sodium: 185 mg

Calories: 213
Fat: 4.5 gm
Cholesterol: 0 mg
Calcium: 83 mg

MAKES ONE 9" x 5" LOAF

Preheat oven to 350°. Spray a 9" x 5" bread pan with nonstick oil.

In a large mixing bowl, combine grated carrots, cranberries, brown sugar, honey, lemon juice, baking soda, oil, poppy seeds and boiling water. Let rest at least 10 minutes.

In a separate bowl, mix together flour, baking powder and cinnamon. After carrot mixture has rested, stir in flour mixture just until moistened, do not overmix. Pour into bread pan. Bake 40 to 50 minutes, or until toothpick inserted in center of bread comes out clean.

Leave in pan 10 minutes longer, then turn out and cool on wire rack. When cool, cut into 12 slices.

The Historic Cranberry

The cranberry got its name from its lovely arched pink and white flowers. Pilgrim settlers thought the flower looked like the beak of the European crane, so they called the fruit "craneberry." However, since the test for freshness is their ability to bounce, they were also called "bounceberries."

Among some Native American nations, the offering of cranberries was a symbol of peace, helping to heal disagreements. Cranberries were so critical to the pilgrims' survival that they wrote laws protecting the plants grown on both public and private lands. New England trading ships carried barrels of the fruit on board to protect against scurvy. And on the Pacific Coast, Oregon settlers harvested the profitable cranberries from their bogs, selling the fruit to California logging and mining camps.

In the early 1800s, Americans began transplanting cranberries, creating cranberry farms, and sharing agricultural knowledge of the valuable fruit. From the north Atlantic Coast, cranberry farms sprang up in the upper midwest and north Pacific Coast. Today, Massachusetts and Wisconsin compete for the title of largest cranberry-producing state. Other major cranberry producers are New Jersey, Washington, Oregon, and in Canada, Ontario, Nova Scotia and British Columbia.

Cranberry Sweet Potatoes

SERVES 4

4 medium-sized sweet
  potatoes
1 cup fresh or dried
  cranberries
½ cup apple juice or cider
¾ cup packed brown sugar
3 tablespoons lemon juice
⅓ cup honey
1 tablespoon melted butter

Serving: 1 Potato
Protein: 2 gm
Carbs: 99 gm
Sodium: 61 mg

Calories: 415
Fat: 3.5 gm
Cholesterol: 8 mg
Calcium: 74 mg

Cut sweet potatoes in half and boil in water until tender. Cool in cold water, then peel off skins. Place potatoes in a baking dish sprayed with nonstick oil.

In a saucepan, combine cranberries, apple juice or cider and brown sugar. Cook 25 minutes. Mix in lemon juice, and spoon cranberry sauce over sweet potatoes. Preheat oven to 325°. Combine honey with melted butter and pour over cranberry sauce. Bake 20 minutes, serve hot from the oven.

Cranberry Vinaigrette

⅓ cup cranberries
2 tablespoons lemon juice
2 tablespoons sugar
¼ cup dry white wine
¼ cup red wine vinegar
2 tablespoons minced parsley
1 clove garlic, minced
pinch of salt
pinch of pepper

MAKES ¾ CUP

Combine all ingredients in blender and process at least 3 minutes. Transfer to glass jar with tight-fitting lid. Refrigerate well before serving.

Serving: 2 Tablespoons
Protein: 0 gm
Carbs: 6 gm
Sodium: 21 mg

Calories: 29
Fat: 0 gm
Cholesterol: 0 mg
Calcium: 7 mg

Cranberry Apple Salad

2 cups fresh cranberries
1 cup water
¾ cup honey
¼ cup sugar
6 medium-sized apples
1 tablespoon lemon juice
5 tablespoons chopped
  walnuts

SERVES 6

Serving: 1/6 Recipe	Calories: 289
Protein: 2 gm	Fat: 4 gm
Carbs: 67 gm	Cholesterol: 0 mg
Sodium: 3 mg	Calcium: 15 mg

In a medium saucepan, put cranberries in water with honey and sugar. Place over medium-high heat until cranberries pop open, about 15 minutes. Remove from heat.

Peel and core apples. Chop into small bite-sized pieces. Sprinkle lemon juice on apples and toss.

While cranberry sauce is still warm, pour over apples and walnuts. Chill at least 1 hour before serving.

Cranberry-Stuffed Haddock

2½ lbs. haddock fillets
½ cup chopped onion
1 tablespoon canola oil
1 tablespoon lemon juice
1 cup cranberries
½ cup packed brown sugar
½ cup orange juice
¼ teaspoon salt
2 tablespoons minced parsley
2 cups cooked white or
    brown rice
1 egg, beaten
1 teaspoon canola oil
1 teaspoon paprika

SERVES 6

Spay a large casserole with nonstick oil. Place half the fillets on bottom of casserole.

Sauté onion in oil. Add lemon juice, cranberries, sugar, orange juice and salt. Simmer 25 minutes.

Preheat oven to 350°. In a mixing bowl, combine cranberry sauce with parsley, cooked rice and beaten egg. Spread mixture over haddock fillets. Place remaining fillets over cranberry mixture. Brush with oil, sprinkle with paprika. Bake 35 minutes.

Serving: 1/6 Recipe	Calories: 366
Protein: 39 gm	Fat: 5.5 gm
Carbs: 39 gm	Cholesterol: 143 mg
Sodium: 245 mg	Calcium: 96 mg

Cranberry BBQ Sauce

MAKES 3½ CUPS

1 cup cranberries
2 cups water
2 teaspoons canola oil
1 medium onion, diced
2 cloves garlic, minced
1½ cups catsup
1 cup red wine
½ cup packed brown sugar
1 teaspoon lemon juice
2 tablespoons
   Worcestershire sauce
2 pinches cayenne
½ teaspoon black pepper

Boil cranberries in water until soft. Drain in fine sieve then mash cranberry pulp through sieve and set aside.

In a large saucepan, sauté onion and garlic in oil. Whisk in cranberry pulp and remaining ingredients. Simmer 30 minutes or until thickened. Store sauce in a sealed jar in the refrigerator.

Serving: 2 Tablespoons   Calories: 96
Protein: 1 gm   Fat: 2 gm
Carbs: 17 gm   Cholesterol: 0 mg
Sodium: 332 mg   Calcium: 20 mg

Cranberried Acorn Squash

2 acorn squash
2 cups fresh or dried
   cranberries
½ cup maple syrup
½ cup packed brown sugar
4 tablespoons frozen orange
   juice concentrate
1 tablespoon softened butter
1 tablespoon cinnamon

Serving: 1/2 Squash
Protein: 2 gm
Carbs: 82 gm
Sodium: 51 mg

Calories: 344
Fat: 3.5 gm
Cholesterol: 8 mg
Calcium: 140 mg

SERVES 4

Preheat oven to 350°. Spray a covered casserole dish with nonstick oil.

Cut squash in half, remove seeds and stringy fibers. Quarter each half and boil until soft. Drain and cool to room temperature. Peel off skins and mash squash in a large bowl.

Mix squash and remaining ingredients. Transfer to casserole dish, cover and bake for 45 minutes.

The Cranberry Harvest

Cranberries are harvested by one of two methods, wet harvesting or dry harvesting. Wet harvesting cranberries requires flooding the cranberry beds with a few inches of water. Using water reels to knock the berries off the plants, the berries float up and are gathered together by a floating boom, wooded slats or floating chains. The berries are then guided onto conveyors belts, slanting up to an open-bed trailer. Moving along the belt, shooting water and puffs of air remove debris, cleaning the cranberries at a rate of about 20,000 pounds an hour. The conveyor belt drops the cranberries into barrels aboard the trailer, each containing 100 pounds of cranberries.

To dry harvest the berries, farmers use cranberry rakes or a special machine with metal-toothed combs. Berries are loaded into sacks, and emptied into metal screens that sift out the leaves and sticks. Cleaned cranberries are packed into crates and hauled out of the bog by helicopter.

At the cranberry processing plant, cranberries are sorted by their ability to bounce down a sloping belt, making their way over one-inch-high boards. A ripe, undamaged cranberry will easily pass the test and be bagged and sold fresh. Those that do not are used in cranberry juice, sauce, jam and tea.

Special Cranberry Relish

1 navel orange
1 lemon
1 lime
1½ cups sugar
3 cups fresh cranberries
¼ cup Grand Marnier

Serving: 2 Tablespoons
Protein: 0 gm
Carbs: 15 gm
Sodium: 0 mg

Calories: 62
Fat: 0 gm
Cholesterol: 0 mg
Calcium: 6 mg

MAKES ABOUT 3½ CUPS

Using a vegetable peeler, peel rind from the orange, lemon and lime. Cut into very thin 1½-inch-long strips. Squeeze juice from the fruit pulps into a bowl.

Put the sugar in a saucepan and cook over moderate heat, stirring until a clear amber syrup forms in about 3 to 4 minutes. Add the citrus rinds, stir in citrus juices and cook 1 minute. Mix in cranberries and bring to a gentle boil. Stirring occasionally, cook until the relish is jam-like, about 15 minutes. Remove from the heat and stir in Grand Marnier. Pour into mold, cool to room temperature, then chill.

Cranberry Walnut Ring

2 cups cranberries
2 cups sugar
1 tablespoon finely
    grated orange rind
3 tablespoons safflower oil
2 teaspoons vanilla
1 egg
2 cups all-purpose flour
2 tablespoons baking powder
½ teaspoon nutmeg
1 teaspoon cinnamon
1 cup skim milk
¼ cup chopped walnuts

Serving: 1 Piece	Calories: 332
Protein: 5 gm	Fat: 6.5 gm
Carbs: 64 gm	Cholesterol: 22 mg
Sodium: 260 mg	Calcium: 140 mg

SERVES 10

Preheat oven to 350°. Spray a bundt pan with nonstick oil.

Process cranberries and sugar in food processor until coarsely chopped. Transfer cranberries to saucepan and cook 5 minutes over low heat, stirring constantly. Remove from heat and add orange rind.

In a mixing bowl, combine oil, vanilla and egg. In a separate bowl, sift together flour, baking powder, nutmeg and cinnamon. Alternately add flour mixture and milk to the cranberry mixture, stirring constantly. Fold in chopped walnuts. Pour batter into pan and bake 45 minutes or until toothpick inserted in center of cake comes out clean. Cool 10 minutes in pan, then turn out onto wire rack to cool.

Apple Cranberry Pie

Pie Shell:
2½ cups all-purpose flour
¼ cup sugar
¼ cup canola oil
½ cup cold skim milk

Filling:
2 cups fresh or dried
   cranberries
3 cups peeled and
   chopped apples
1 cup golden raisins
3 tablespoons chopped
   walnuts
1 tablespoon cinnamon
1 teaspoon ground cloves
2 cups sugar

Top:
1 teaspoon skim milk
1 tablespoon sugar

Serving: 1 Piece	Calories: 572
Protein: 7 gm	Fat: 9.5 gm
Carbs: 120 gm	Cholesterol: 0 mg
Sodium: 14 mg	Calcium: 57 mg

MAKES ONE 8-PIECE PIE

Preheat oven to 350°. Spray a 9-inch pie plate with nonstick oil.

Sift flour and sugar together. In a separate bowl, combine oil and milk. Pour liquid into flour, blend with fork, wrap in plastic and chill 15 minutes. Divide dough into 2 parts. Between sheets of waxed paper, roll one piece of dough round and one rectangular. Place round piece in pie pan. Cut rectangular dough into ½-inch strips and cover with waxed paper.

Simmer cranberries in saucepan with boiling water for 5 minutes and drain. Combine cranberries with remaining filling ingredients. Pour into pie shell. Weave lattice top with ½-inch strips of dough. Gently brush top with milk, sprinkle with sugar. Bake for 50 minutes until golden brown.

Cranberry-Pear Chutney

MAKES ABOUT 4 CUPS

2 tablespoons canola oil
1 large yellow onion,
    finely diced
2 jalapeño peppers, diced
1½ cups red or white wine
    vinegar
1 cup packed brown sugar
½ teaspoon cinnamon
1 teaspoon ground ginger
1 teaspoon ground cardamom
1 teaspoon cumin
2 cloves minced garlic
2 cups cranberries
2 lbs. firm ripe pears, peeled,
    cored and finely diced

In a saucepan, sauté onion and jalapeños in oil over medium heat until onion is clear. Add vinegar, brown sugar, spices and garlic. Bring to a simmer, then add cranberries. Stirring frequently, simmer until the cranberries start to burst, then add pears. Cook 5 minutes more.

Ladle the chutney into hot sterilized jars with tight-fitting lids. Process in hot water bath for 10 minutes.

Serving: 2 Tablespoons	Calories: 57
Protein: 0 gm	Fat: 1 gm
Carbs: 13 gm	Cholesterol: 0 mg
Sodium: 3 mg	Calcium: 12 mg

Cranberry Lemon Custard

Cranberry Sauce:
1½ cups cranberries
1 cup orange juice
1 cup packed brown sugar
½ teaspoon cinnamon

Custard:
2 cups skim milk
1 cup cold skim evaporated milk
1 cup sugar
3 tablespoons cornstarch
pinch of salt
1 egg, beaten
1 egg white, beaten
1 tablespoon finely grated lemon zest
2 tablespoons fresh lemon juice
pinch of nutmeg

Serving: 1 Custard
Protein: 8 gm
Carbs: 90 gm
Sodium: 146 mg
Calories: 394
Fat: 1 gm
Cholesterol: 38 mg
Calcium: 270 mg

SERVES 6

Simmer cranberry sauce ingredients in covered saucepan until thick.

In a small saucepan, scald skim milk. Boil water in bottom pan of double boiler and pour scalded milk into top pan. In a small bowl, blend evaporated milk with sugar, cornstarch and salt. Stirring constantly, slowly add evaporated milk mixture to scalded milk. Continue stirring over boiling water 20 minutes. Remove top pan and whisk in beaten eggs. Replace top pan over water, and stirring constantly, cook 10 minutes more. Remove from heat, cool 10 minutes, then stir in grated lemon rind, juice and nutmeg.

In 6 tall glass custard dishes or mugs, ladle alternating layers of lemon custard and cranberry sauce. Chill well.

Cranberry Jelly

4 cups cranberries
2 cups boiling water
1 cinnamon stick
2 whole cloves
2 cups sugar

Serving: 2 Tablespoons   Calories: 110
Protein: 0 gm   Fat: 0 gm
Carbs: 28 gm   Cholesterol: 0 mg
Sodium: 1 mg   Calcium: 3 mg

MAKES ABOUT 16 OZ.

Wash and clean cranberries. Place in saucepan with boiling water, cinnamon stick and cloves. Boil for 4 minutes, until the cranberry skins burst. Press liquid and fruit through strainer, discarding skins and spices.

Stir sugar into cranberry purée. Return to saucepan and bring to a boil. Simmer 7 minutes if fresh cranberries were firm, or 5 minutes if they were soft.

Skim froth off top. Pour liquid into wet, sterilized jelly jars. Seal according to manufacturer's instructions.

Cranberry Punch

2 cups sparkling mineral
    water, chilled
2 cups peach nectar, chilled
2 cups orange juice, chilled
3 cups cranberry juice
1 tablespoon lemon juice
orange slices

SERVES 8

Combine all ingredients in a large pitcher. Pour over ice cubes in serving glasses. Garnish with orange slices.

Serving: 1 Cup
Protein: 1 gm
Carbs: 29 gm
Sodium: 7 mg

Calories: 116
Fat: 0 gm
Cholesterol: 0 mg
Calcium: 21 mg